Jesus' Parables About Priorities

James W. Moore

JESUS'

Parables About Priorities

ABINGDON PRESS

NASHVILLE

JESUS' PARABLES ABOUT PRIORITIES

This book is printed on acid-free paper.

Library of Congress Cataloging-in-Publication Data
Moore, James W. (James Wendell), 1938–
  Jesus' parables about priorities / James W. Moore.
    p.   cm.
ISBN 978-0-687-65094-1 (binding: adhesive perfect : alk. paper)
1. Jesus Christ—Parables. 2. Christian life. I. Title.
  BT375.3.M663   2008
226.8'06—dc22

2008004668

10 11 12 13 14 15 16 17—10 9 8 7 6 5 4

MANUFACTURED IN THE UNITED STATES OF AMERICA

For our grandchildren,
Sarah, Paul, Dawson, Daniel, and Mason,
who are learning every day
how important right priorities are
and how Jesus helps us sort things out

CONTENTS

INTRODUCTION

Why did Jesus use parables, and how do we unravel them and discover their timeless and powerful messages? Let me begin by giving you five key ideas that help unlock the truths found in all the parables of Jesus.

First, Jesus spoke in parables—short stories that teach a faith lesson—to be understood and remembered, to proclaim the good news, and to make people think.

Second, Jesus saw himself as one who came to serve the needy, and he believed that the kingdom of God existed anywhere kingdom-deeds such as love, mercy, kindness, and compassion were being done.

Third, God's love for us is unconditional; and God wants us to love one another like that—unconditionally.

Fourth, one way to discover the central truth of a parable is to look for the surprise in it. Look for the moment when you lift your eyebrows, or the moment when the original hearers of the story probably thought or said in surprise—or maybe even shock—"Oh my goodness, did you hear that?"

Fifth, it's important to remember that parables are designed to convey one central truth. Parables (as opposed to allegories, in which everything in the story has a symbolic meaning) make one main point.

Parables slip up on us. They flip our values. They turn our world upside down. They surprise us. This is the great thing about the parables of Jesus: They are always relevant and always personal. They speak eloquently to you and me, here and now. In this book, we will examine six of Jesus' thought-provoking parables about priorities to see if we can find ourselves, and God's truth for us, in these magnificent truth-stories. They are, after all, truth-stories for us—truth-stories from the mind of Jesus that can change our lives as they proclaim God's truth for you and me.

1

The Priority of Love
"Looking for Love in All the Wrong Places"

Scripture: Luke 15:11-32

It took Alex Haley twelve years to do it, twelve years to research it and write it. But finally in 1976, he completed his book. It was titled *Roots: The Saga of an American Family*.

In this epic work, which some believe is destined to become a classic of American literature, Alex Haley traces his family's origins back to their "roots" in a two-century drama beginning with the African Kunta Kinte, continuing through the six generations that came after him, and concluding with Alex Haley.

Roots also helped usher in a new era in television as millions of Americans watched the graphic portrayal of a novel on prime-time television. Our family watched as many of the episodes together as we could—and we discussed them. During the last television segment, there was a powerful and poignant scene. Tom Moore, the son of "Chicken George," is preparing to take his family to freedom in Tennessee when Evan Brent, who has treated them so terribly, comes out to try to stop them. Brent has cursed them, beaten them, abused them, and overworked them with horrendous cruelty, especially Tom. Brent always seemed to have it in for Tom, and, on at least one occasion, he flogged Tom almost to death with a whip.

In the scene where Brent tries to stop them, the slaves, with the thirst for freedom in their hearts, turn on him. They capture Brent, tie him to the whipping post, and bring a whip to Tom so Tom can pay Brent back for the brutalizing things he has done. Brent whimpers and pleads for mercy. Brent—the one who has been so cruel, so hateful, so mean to them—now pleads for mercy.

Holding the whip tightly in his hand, Tom looks at Brent tied to the whipping post. He hears Brent whimpering and begging for compassion. If ever a man deserved to be flogged, it was Brent. Here was Tom's chance to get back at him. Here was Tom's chance to unleash two centuries of his family's hurt and heartache and frustration. And yet, as our family watched that scene together, I found myself uneasy and saying out loud: "I hope he doesn't whip him. I'm going to be disappointed if he beats him." Our daughter said, "Don't worry, Dad, he won't, it just wouldn't fit his character. It wouldn't fit his personality." And she was right. Just about that time, Tom drops the whip to the ground and turns and walks away. He refuses to beat Brent. Brent falls to his knees at the whipping post and cries in relief. I felt relieved too. I would have been let down if Tom had beaten him. Tom had been there. He knew what it felt like, and in that tense moment, compassion had won the day. I thought to myself, "That is beautiful; the quality of mercy is indeed beautiful. It is so much better than vengeance or hostility." Then I realized that that is precisely what Jesus believed, taught, lived for, what he died for, and what he rose again to show us— that mercy is better than vengeance, that love is better than hate.

Since that time, I have realized even more deeply something very important. Namely, that the best qualities we know in life are reflections of God. Let me express that again: the best qualities we know in life are reflections of God. The best attitudes we see and feel and know and express in this life are reflections of the spirit of God.

For example, we know from our own personal experience that some attitudes are better than others. The word *better* here may mean more "Godlike." To say love is better than hate, mercy is better than cruelty, empathy is better than jealousy, is just another way of saying that love, mercy, and empathy are of God; they are more Godlike. Thus, when we express these kinds of attitudes, we are at that moment reflecting God.

In 1 Corinthians 13:13, when Paul said, "The greatest of these is love," he meant that the most Godlike thing in the world is love. And this is what Jesus is showing us graphically in the parable of the prodigal son as he paints the picture of a loving father whose attitudes and qualities are reflections of God. Jesus is saying, "This is what God is like." Here in this parable, we see a father who is kind, patient, compassionate, tender, forgiving, merciful, understanding, and loving. Jesus brings out the greatness of these qualities even more dramatically by setting them over against the backdrop of the elder brother, who is jealous and resentful, spiteful and unbending, harsh and vindictive.

There is no question about who is reflecting God in this story. The father is. There is no question about which qualities depicted in the parable are in keeping with the character of God in this great parable. Jesus is saying, "This is what God is like, and this is what God wants us to be like." Don't miss this now, the father is gracious and merciful, and he wants his older son to be gracious and merciful too. The father reflects the love of God, but the elder brother misses it and, instead, reflects bitterness and pettiness. That's the way it works. Every time you and I perform an act of love or kindness, we are reflecting God, and when we fail to be thoughtful or patient or tender, we are blocking God, opposing God, hindering God. Let's look at this more closely by being more specific.

First, Compassion Is Better Than Condemnation, So It Must Be More Godlike

Compassion is a reflection of God. This is seen vividly in the prodigal son parable. The father is the picture of compassion while the elder brother angrily points the accusing, condemning finger. No quality is more beautiful than compassion; no attitude is more reflective of God.

One clear admonition that leaps out of this passage is this: be more compassionate. If you want to be like God, start here. Be more compassionate. To be compassionate means to get into another person's shoes. Oh, how we need this great attribute in all of our relationships! Recently, I saw an article for teenagers titled "How to Raise Your Parents." It contained six tongue-in-cheek suggestions for being more compassionate toward your parents. It read like this:

1. Do not be afraid to speak their language. Try using strange-sounding phrases like, "I'll help you with the dishes," and "Yes."

2. Try to understand their music. Play a tape or a CD of one of their favorite tunes until you are accustomed to the sound.

3. Be patient with the underachiever. When you catch your dieting dad sneaking salted peanuts, do not show your disapproval. Tell him you like fat dads.

4. Encourage your parents to talk about their problems. Try to keep in mind that to them things like earning a living

and paying off the mortgage seem important.

5. Be tolerant of their appearance. When your dad gets a hair cut, do not feel personally humiliated. Remember, it is important to him to look like his peers.

6. Most of all: If they do something wrong, let them know it is their behavior you dislike, not themselves. Remember, parents need to feel they are loved.
(http://susquehannachurchofchrist.org/bulletin/2000/06-18-00.html#HOW%20TO%20RAISE%20YOUR. Accessed January 16, 2008.)

In a lighthearted way, that writer is saying something very important. Namely, that we would all be better off if there were more compassion, patience, and understanding in the world. Remember how Jesus said, "Whoever has seen me has seen the Father" (John 14:9). And then remember how compassionately he dealt with the woman caught in adultery. The mob was ready to stone her to death. But not Jesus. He wanted no part in condemning people. His was a heart of compassion. He said, "Neither do I condemn you. Go your way, and from now on do not sin again" (John 8:11).

When you read the New Testament, one thing is sure: compassion (not condemnation) is a reflection of God.

Second, Forgiveness Is Better Than Resentment, So It Must Be More Godlike

The forgiving spirit is a dramatic reflection of God. Anybody can be hostile, anybody can be bitter, anybody can be vengeful, but it takes a Godlike person to forgive. Look again at the prodigal son parable. The father is quick to forgive—he doesn't even have to be asked. He runs down the road to meet his wayward son; he interrupts his confession. He calls for a great celebration. The relationship is restored that quickly because the father was anxious to love, eager to reconcile, quick to forgive.

But notice how the elder brother was quick to resent, quick to get angry, quick to feel hostility, quick to criticize, quick to feel self-pity, quick to point the finger. Don't you feel sorry for people like that? Wouldn't that be a miserable existence?

The forgiving spirit is so much better, so much more fulfilling, so much more Godlike than the destructive, poisonous spirit of resentment. If this parable says anything to us, it says that God is forgiving and that he wants us to be forgiving.

When we read the New Testament, one thing is sure, namely, that forgiveness, not resentment, is a reflection of God, and every time we forgive or encourage forgiveness we are putting our weight down on the side of God.

Third, Redeeming Love Is Better Than Destructive Hate, So It Must Be of God; It Must Be More Godlike

Redeeming love, a love that works to help and heal must be a reflection of God. Every good parent knows about the power and potential of redeeming love. Every good parent knows that the best way to get your children to do and be the right thing is to love them into it. You may be able to use force for a while, but it won't last; the only way to really win your children over is to love them. Abraham Lincoln was criticized for not being tough enough on the enemy. People said, "Mr. President, you must destroy your enemies." Don't you love Lincoln's answer: "Do I not destroy my enemies when I make them my friends?"

Now, how does that relate to the parable of the prodigal son? Maybe like this: maybe this father was so thankful to God for his son that he had a heart of redeeming love, even though the son had done wrong; even though the son had run away, he knew that his father had a heart of redeeming love, so he knew that he could come back home. That was very unusual because, back then, if a son ran away from home, he was considered dead. He was written off. He was not to be talked about or spoken of, and, if someone did forget and mention his name, the father was supposed to quickly say, "He is dead to me." And yet this son knew that customs and traditions didn't really matter because his father had a heart of redeeming love—and he was right. He didn't have to win him back over. All he had to do was come home. The father was waiting with open arms.

That son had been looking for love in all the wrong places. Finally, he realized that real love was right there on his own doorstep. It had been there all along, wrapped up in a gracious father who knew full well that compassion is better than condemnation, that forgiveness is better than resentment, and that redeeming love is better than destructive hate.

The point is clear: The father is loving, and he wants the elder brother to be loving too; indeed, he wants all of his children—he wants us—to live in that gracious, loving spirit.

Dietrich Bonhoeffer once said that, in Jesus, the message and the messenger were one. That's our calling too: to tell the message and to be the message, to be compassionate, forgiving, and loving.

2
The Priority of Grace
"Amazing Grace"

Scripture: Luke 15:11-32

Shel Silverstein wrote it in 1964. It's a children's story called *The Giving Tree*, and it has become a favorite of children (of all ages) for more than forty years now. The story tells of a tree that loved a little boy unconditionally and sacrificially over many years. In the beginning, the boy loves to climb on the tree and swing from her branches and gather her leaves and sleep in her shade, and this brings great joy to the giving tree.

But as the years go by, the boy grows older, and he no longer wants to play in and around and under the tree. Rather, he wants to buy things. He wants money, so the tree gives him her apples, so he can sell them and make money. And, again, giving her apples to the boy makes the tree happy.

But the boy goes off and stays away for a very long time, and the tree misses him so much and is sad. When he finally returns, the tree is overjoyed, but this time the boy tells her that he is too busy to play there. He wants a house. Graciously and happily, the giving tree gives him her branches so he can use them to build a house. The boy takes the branches and goes away for a long time again.

Later, he comes back, and this time he wants a boat. The tree tells him to cut down her trunk and to use it to make a boat. He does so and sails away.

More time passes, and then the boy returns and has grown very old and is looking for a quiet place to sit and rest. The tree tells him that an old stump is a great place to sit and rest. The boy accepts her invitation and sits on her stump, and this makes the tree very happy.

The giving tree was a very special tree. She was special not because she was so tall that she reached high into the clouds like the trees in East Texas. She was special not because her trunk was so huge that cars could be driven through her tummy like the trees in Northern California. She was special not because she possessed certain leaves or exotic fruit that could be found on no other tree. She was just a common, everyday apple tree.

No, this tree was special because she gave so much of herself away. No matter what the boy needed, the tree was always ready to share. Eventually, she gave all of herself away in love. That was her greatness. She was "the giving tree"; she was a tree full of grace. Amazing grace.

In the Christian church, we talk a lot about grace. It is the major emblem of the Christian faith. Amazing grace—that's what the cross is about! It's what the New Testament is about. It's what the gospel is about. We preach it from our pulpits. We sing it in our hymns. We thank God for it in our prayers. We try to live it in our lives. Amazing grace! But what in the world is it? Well, obviously it is a very special kind of love, a special kind of "giving tree" love.

One of the most beautiful pictures of grace in the Scriptures is found in the parable of the prodigal son. In this magnificent parable (which has been called, appropriately, "The Greatest Short Story Ever Told") Jesus is showing us two very important things. First, what God is like, and second, what God wants us to be like. And in both instances the word is *grace*. In the story, the father is gracious, and (don't miss this now) he wants his children to be gracious like him.

Remember the story: a man has two sons. The younger son gets restless. He demands his inheritance early, converts it into cash, and arrogantly heads out for the far country to be his own boss and to do his own thing. He squanders his money, falls on hard times, sees the error and selfishness of his ways, is penitent, and decides to return home. Earlier, he left in arrogance. Now he returns in humility, wanting and needing forgiveness but knowing that he doesn't deserve it.

The father sees him coming. (We get the feeling that the father has looked hopefully down that road a thousand times.) The father runs to greet him and welcome him home. The father is so overjoyed that he calls for a great feast to receive the prodigal home in a celebrative way and to include him again in the family circle. So, they have a big party, and they all live happily ever after. No! Not quite. The elder brother doesn't like this one bit. He is jealous, angry, resentful, and he refuses to go in. He refuses to participate, and, in the process, he makes himself look bad. His pettiness is exposed in all of its ugliness by the brilliant light of the father's forgiving, loving spirit through God's amazing grace. The point is clear: God is full of grace like that father. God is gracious like that father, and he wants his children to be gracious too.

God gives us this amazing grace, and he wants us to live in that spirit. He wants us to be gracious and forgiving and loving like him.

> Amazing Grace how sweet the sound
> That saved a wretch like me!
> I once was lost, but now am found
> Was blind but now I see.

That's how the hymn writer put it, but let me try to define it more specifically. Grace—what is it? Try these thoughts on for size.

First, Grace Means Undeserved Love

Undeserved love, unmerited favor, unearned forgiveness, the prodigal did nothing to deserve this gracious welcome. It was a gift freely given! He was received, restored, redeemed, reconciled, not because of anything he did but because of the father's loving touch.

Myra Brooks Welch's beloved poem about the violin auctioneer expresses it well:

'Twas battered and scarred, and the
    auctioneer
Thought it scarcely worth his while
To waste much time on the old violin,
But held it up with a smile.
"What am I bidden, good folks," he cried,
"Who'll start the bidding for me?"
"A dollar, a dollar"; then "Two! Only two?
Two dollars, who'll make it three?
Three dollars, once; three dollars, twice;
Going for three—" But no,
From the room, far back, a gray-haired
    man
Came forward and picked up the bow;
Then, wiping the dust from the old violin,
And tightening the loose strings,
He played a melody pure and sweet
As a caroling angel sings.

The music ceased, and the auctioneer,
With a voice that was quiet and low,
Said: "What am I bid for the old violin?"
And he held it up with the bow.
"A thousand dollars, and who'll make it
    two?
Two thousand! And who'll make it three?
Three thousand, once; three thousand,
    twice,
And going, and gone," said he.
The people cheered, but some of them
    cried,

"We do not quite understand
What changed its worth." Swift came the
   reply:
"The touch of a master's hand."

And many a man with life out of tune,
And battered and scarred with sin,
Is auctioned cheap to the thoughtless
   crowd,
Much like the old violin.
A "mess of pottage," a glass of wine;
A game—and he travels on.
He is "going" once, and "going" twice,
He's "going" and almost "gone."
But the Master comes, and the foolish
   crowd
Never can quite understand
The worth of a soul and the change that's
   wrought
By the touch of the Master's hand.
(Originally published by Brethren Press)

That is the picture of grace, isn't it? We (like the prodigal) are received into the circle of God's love not because we are good, but because He is good, not because we are great, but because He is gracious. We are made whole by the touch of the Master's hand. Grace, then, first of all is undeserved love.

Second, Grace Is Unconditional Love

The father's love for the prodigal had no conditions, no strings attached! Remember the legend about the young man proposing to his girlfriend. He said: "You are the only one for me. I love you and you alone. No one else could ever do. Will you marry me?" The girl answered, "Am I really worthy of you? My sister is so much more beautiful than I am. Perhaps you should marry her. She is in the next room." The young man went into the next room to check this out. In a moment, he returned and said, "Your sister is not nearly as beautiful as you are! You lied to me!" "No!" said the girl, "You lied to me because if you had truly loved me as you said, you never would have gone to look!"

Grace is love that will not waver, love that will not bend. It is love that says, "There is nothing or no one in all the world that will stop me from loving you." Grace is unconditional love.

Third, Grace Means Unending Love

The father did not put the prodigal on a time schedule. He didn't say, "Well, I'll forgive him if he comes back before the end of the month." The door is always open. The welcome mat is always ready. The loving arms are always available.

My friend, Mark Trotter, wrote a delightful article some years ago on the theology of baseball that speaks to this. He said:

> The genius of the game of baseball, and the most delightful theological insight is that there is always grace.... Nobody's record is very good. The better players only succeed in doing what they get paid to do about one-third of the time they try to do it. Think of what it would be like in your job if your performance record was like that. On a scale of ten, if your performance record never got over a three, you'd get fired. In baseball, if you get a three, they'll give you a million-dollar contract. And put you in the hall of fame.
>
> The most gracious part of the structure of baseball is that it has no clock. Baseball is the only major sport that isn't governed by the ineluctable sweep of time. In baseball, time is always on your side. One of the great theologians of baseball, Yogi Berra, put it this way: "It ain't over 'til it's over!" ...
>
> In 1986, the third baseman for the San Francisco Giants, Bob Brenley, set a major league record with four errors in one

game, at third base, against the Atlanta
Braves. And then at his last bat in the
ninth inning, the count was 3 and 2, and
he hit a home run and won the game 7 to
6. (From goat to hero with one swing of
the bat.) That is why it's never over 'til it's
over. And that's what grace means. Grace
means you'll always have another chance.
Life doesn't erase your errors or your sins,
but you are given a chance to live as if
they weren't there. (Mark Trotter, FUMC,
San Diego, March 22, 1987)

Grace is undeserved love, unconditional
love, unending love.

Finally, Grace Is Unselfish Love

When the prodigal returned home, the father
didn't demand his pound of flesh, he didn't
scream about his rights, he didn't even give a
parental lecture. He just rejoiced graciously and
unselfishly in the safe return of his son. He was
a giving tree! There is no selfishness in grace;
there is only self-giving love!

When Tex Evans first started out in the
ministry he served a church in a small
Texas town. One of his neighbors was
a man named Mr. Gentry. Tex Evans

noticed that Mr. Gentry worked in his yard a lot . . . and that he always whistled while he worked. He would work with the roses in the front yard, whistling away. Then he would move to the side yard and work with his tulips . . . still whistling. When he went to the back yard to work in the vegetable garden, he would whistle even louder. . . .

One day at the country store in the middle of the little town, Tex mentioned something about the whistling Mr. Gentry. One of the old-timers asked, "Do you know why Mr. Gentry always whistles when he is outside in the yard?" Tex replied that he had no idea. The old-timer said quietly, "His wife is blind." It was then that Tex understood why Mr. Gentry always whistled. His whistling was a message to Mrs. Gentry, "I am out here, Dear . . . now I'm over here . . . now I'm in the back yard. If you need me, call and I will hear you. I'm not far away; I'm not going to leave you alone." (William Jenkins, "The Whistler," www.lcnews.us/religion072006.htm. Accessed January 9, 2008)

God is whistling for us right now. He whistles from a cross (if you will, from a giving tree), and the tune he is whistling is "Amazing Grace."

3

The Priority of Being Prepared
"When Crisis Comes"

Scripture: Matthew 25:1-13

Some years ago, a man came to my office. He was deeply troubled. It was obvious. He said, "Jim, I need to talk. I feel so empty, so dried up inside. I'm scared and lonely." He paused for a moment, looked at the floor, and then he continued. He said, "I have just come from my doctor's office. He tells me that I have a terminal illness. I have six months, maybe a year, to live." Then he added, "As that news sunk in, I realized that I have no spiritual resources, no spiritual strength to face this. I have nothing to fall back on, nothing to lean on." He said, "Some people think I'm wealthy, and, materially, I am, but that doesn't matter now, does it?"

"Really and truly," he said, "I'm poor in the things that count most. I see it now. All these years, I have put my faith in the wrong things. The truth is: I am spiritually destitute!" He paused again, and then as if he were thinking out loud, he said, "You know, I could pick up that phone and call any bank in this city and borrow any amount of money to do whatever I wanted— just on my name, I could borrow..." His voice trailed off. He leaned over and put his head in his hands. Then very quietly, he whispered, "I guess there are some things you just can't borrow!"

I encouraged him as much as I could, promised to stay close to him, and prayed with him. After he left, I found myself thinking of a parable that Jesus told long ago that underscores the very truth that man had run head-on into that day, namely, when crisis comes, there are some things you cannot borrow!

The story, which is found in the Gospel of Matthew (25:1-13), is about an incident at a wedding celebration. It is called the parable of the wise and foolish maidens or the parable on preparedness.

You remember, of course, from your study of the New Testament that a wedding party was one of the greatest of all festivities in a Palestinian village. Everybody turned out. Men got off work. Children were let out of their synagogue school, women put aside their household chores, and all went to the wedding and remained for the celebration.

The high point of the wedding came when the groom took his new bride from her father's house to their new home. Here's how it worked: first, there was the ceremony; next, the bride and groom would go to the house of the bride's father to negotiate the dowry; then, on to a joyous party. Here is where the parable picks up. The young neighborhood girls are waiting for the groom to bring his bride home. But, there is an unexpected, long delay, and the girls fall asleep. Then at midnight there is a shout. The girls wake up. It's the announcement that the big moment is near. "Get ready! Get ready! Won't be long now! The bride and groom will be coming out very shortly." However, in the story, some of the young girls who have been waiting for this crucial moment in the wedding celebration now have a big problem. They had not anticipated the delay. They had not counted on a problem. They had not prepared in advance well enough. And now, they have run short of oil for their lamps.

Hastily, they try to borrow some, but cannot, so they rush off to get more oil only to find, on their return, that they missed it, that the big moment has passed, that the celebration is over, and that they missed out because they were not adequately prepared!

The point is clear: when crisis comes, you better have prepared ahead, because there are some things you can't borrow! When those crucial moments come, you have to take responsibility for your own life. It's good to have "borrowing power." It's good to have material wealth. It's good to have friends to lean on, but sometimes you have to stand alone, sometimes you have to stand on your own two feet.

The businessman who came to my office that day had learned it the hard way. Jesus had taught it long ago: when crisis comes, there are some things you just can't borrow.

Here are a few examples.

First, When Crisis Comes, You Cannot Borrow a Spirit of Inner Poise

Confidence

Poise, confidence, balance, assurance, stability, control—whatever you want to call it—you can't borrow that. It has to be cultivated and grown, and when crisis comes, it serves you well.

Spiritual poise comes from spending time with God. It is quite simply the confidence, the blessed assurance, that God is with us in every circumstance of life and even beyond this life. So, we don't have to run scared or be afraid. We can be poised, because God is with us, and he loves us like a father. But, you can't borrow that. You have to grow your own. Kipling put it well in his poem "If," which begins like this:

> If you can keep your head when all about
>   you
> Are losing theirs and blaming it on you;
> If you can trust yourself when all men
>   doubt you,
> But make allowance for their doubting
>   too;
>
> If you can wait and not be tired by
>   waiting,
> Or being lied about, don't deal in lies,
> Or being hated, don't give way to hating
> And yet don't look too good, nor talk too
>   wise.
>
> If you can dream—and not make dreams
>   your master;
> If you can think—and not make thoughts
>   your aim;
> If you can meet with Triumph and
>   Disaster

and treat those two imposters just the
    same;

If you can bear to hear the truth you've
    spoken
Twisted by knaves to make a trap for
    fools,
Or watch the things you gave your life to
    broken,
And stoop and build 'em up with wornout
    tools.

Now, that's it! The spirit of inner poise! And
you can't borrow that! It only comes from
knowing who you are and whose you are, what
you believe and what you are committed to. It
only comes from hours and hours of fellowship
with God and his people.

Second, When Crisis Comes, You Cannot Borrow the Bible

Of course, you could borrow someone's copy
of the Bible, but when trouble comes, you need
your own Bible; you need the Scriptures inside
of you, written indelibly on your heart. You
need your own Bible that you can read daily,
marking passages that have special meaning for
you, writing your thoughts in the margins.

I admit to you that when I try to use someone else's Bible, it seems very strange to me. I feel like an alien in a foreign land. I have much more difficulty finding certain passages. But with my own Bible, I feel at home. I feel like I'm visiting with a trusted friend. What about you? Are you at home in the Scriptures? Are you on good terms with your Bible? Is it a friend or a stranger? When crisis comes, you need a friend!

In desperation, people have turned to the Bible for strength, for comfort, for the word of life, and sometimes they have come up empty because they didn't know how to find its treasures.

Edward Blair, in his book *The Bible and You* (Nashville: Abingdon, 1953, p. 52), points out:

> The person who is looking for a way to master the Bible in 3 easy lessons will be disappointed. In the first place, one can never "master" the Bible, one can only be mastered by it. In the second place, the Bible is so immeasurably rich that the human mind cannot possibly embrace it all in a few attempts at understanding....Familiarity with the Bible comes only by long exposure...to its contents...coming to it with an open, alert

mind, respecting the individuality of the writers and the inspiration of God, trying to understand what the words meant then and what they mean to us now, reading in historical context and applying those truths to our own lives today.

When you see it like that, you realize that you could no more hastily borrow the Bible in time of crisis than those young girls in Jesus' parable could hastily borrow oil for their lamps.

Remember the old story about the minister who was visiting one evening in the home of some of his church members? They asked him a question about where something was located in the Scriptures. He asked if he could see their Bible. The mother asked their little four-year-old daughter, Jennie, to "go into the den to the coffee table and bring our favorite book, the one we love most of all, the one we read all the time." Jennie ran out and in a moment came back with the Macy's catalog!

Now, let me ask you something. What is the favorite book in your home? What is the one you love most of all and read all the time? Be honest now. How long has it been? How long has it been since you spent some time with your Bible?

Third, When Crisis Comes, You Can't Borrow a Prayer Life

Just this week as I was walking to my car on the church parking lot, a dear lady who is a devoted member of our church came up to me and said: "Jim, I just want you to know that I have been praying for you." "Thank you, but why?" I said to her. "Have I been doing something wrong?" "Oh, no! Not that," she responded with a warm smile. "It's just that you are my minister, and I love you, and I'm praying for you!"

We all need that, don't we? The prayers of others, the prayers of those who love us. But, we also need our own prayer life. In fact, I have learned in my own life, that when I have difficulty praying, that it is a sure-fire warning signal to me that I may be drifting away from God and away from the faith. A good prayer life is something we all need, and it's something we can't borrow.

I read recently about a little boy who was losing patience with God because he misunderstood what prayer is. He said: "Now look, Lord, Aunt Stella isn't married yet; Uncle Hubert hasn't got a job; and Daddy's hair is still falling out. I'm tired of saying prayers for this family without getting any results!" Put that over against the little girl who prayed: "Oh, God, bless mommy and daddy and me. And, dear God, please take care of yourself, 'cause if anything should happen to you, we would all be in a fix!"

That is real prayer: being with God and recognizing how important he is in our lives. And you can't borrow that!

Fourth, When Crisis Comes, You Can't Borrow the Church

Now, of course, people do borrow the church buildings for weddings and funerals and meetings. We offer it gladly, but there is something very sad to me about people who, having no church, come to borrow one, for all that they can borrow is a physical structure. They can't really borrow the church, for what makes the church "the church" can't be loaned out.

To worship there, to sing together, to laugh, to witness, to serve, to kneel at the altar, to know that love, to feel that acceptance and support and encouragement, to feel God's presence there, to see him in others, to be a part of Christ's continuing ministry, to be a part of that rich heritage, to feel God's touch through his people, to be reminded of the priorities of life— I need that every day! Oh, how I need that!

Especially, I need it when crisis comes! I can't tell you how much I love the church!

R. H. Nelson was one of the finest and most devoted church men I have ever known. He was the Sunday school superintendent at Shreveport First Church for more than thirty years. When he was in his seventies, he began to have little spells with his heart. One weekday morning, I walked into the sanctuary and found Mr. Nelson sitting on the kneeling pad at the altar rail. He was holding his chest and having difficulty breathing. I rushed over to him. When he saw me, he said: "It's all right, Jim. I'm just having one of my little heart attacks. I've taken my medicine, and I'll be OK in a minute. Don't worry." I said, "Mr. Nelson, you are gonna die down here at this church one of these days." With a weak smile, Mr. Nelson said, "Wouldn't that be wonderful?"

Now, let me tell you something, you can borrow the church building, but you can't borrow that kind of churchmanship.

Finally, When Crisis Comes, You Can't Borrow a Personal Commitment of Faith

Each of us must find his or her own faith. Here is how an anonymous poet of the fifteenth century put it:

You will know him when he comes
Not by any din of drums
Nor the vantage of his airs
Nor by anything he wears
Neither by his crown
Nor his gown
But his presence known shall be
By the holy harmony
Which his coming makes in thee.

Do you know that holy harmony? You can't borrow that! It only comes from a personal encounter with the living Lord.

Let me conclude with this: A man once came to a farmer and asked to be taken on as a hired hand. "What can you do?" the farmer asked him. The man replied, "I can sleep when the wind blows!" The farmer thought that was a strange answer, but he needed a worker, so, with some reservations, he went on and hired the man. A couple of weeks later, as the farmer was falling asleep, a storm came up. Winds were blowing and lashing. The farmer woke up and heard the winds, and he remembered the broken barn door, the weak place in the fence, and some ripped wire in the chicken coop. Concerned about his stock, he got up and went out into the storm to check on them. And what do you think he found? The barn door, the fence, and the chicken coop had all been repaired. The animals were all safe. And the hired worker was sleeping soundly. Then the farmer remembered what he had said, "I can sleep when the wind blows." He could sleep because he had prepared for the storm! Can you?

4

The Priority of Courage
"Locked in a Room with Open Doors"

Scripture: Matthew 25:14-30

Some years ago while leading a youth retreat, I asked the young people there to anonymously complete this open-ended sentence: "Being a teenager in today's world is like..."

How would you complete that sentence? What is it really like to be a teenager today? Well, their responses were remarkable and revealing. For example, one wrote this: "Being a teenager in today's world is like soaring through space in a rocket ship, knowing all the right buttons to push but, somehow, being unable to push them."

Another completed the sentence like this: "Being a teenager in today's world is like standing in the wings of a great theatre called life, wanting so much to go out on stage and be a big hit but feeling so paralyzed by stage fright."

Another wrote this: "Being a teenager in today's world is like being a young bird and wanting to spread my wings and fly but scared—scared to try—scared to leave the safety of my warm, secure nest."

And one said: "Being a teenager in today's world is like being locked in a room with open doors."

In these poignant sentences, we hear a recurring theme that is common not only to young people but, indeed, to people of all ages. We have all felt it: the intense longing to step out on our own and to really taste life but being somehow afraid to take the plunge, or the excitement of incredible possibilities but being frozen by fear.

Can we relate to this? Do we have fears or attitudes or weaknesses that imprison us? Crippling anxieties that cut us off from life, from other people, from God? Are we really free to live fully and abundantly and radiantly as God intended? Or are we locked in a room with open doors? One teenager expressed it like this:

I want to touch you, world, but I'm afraid of being burnt and I'm afraid of being bitten and I'm afraid of being touched back...perhaps too deeply or too suddenly and I will never be the same again. I want to touch you, world, but I'm afraid of reaching out too soon and I'm afraid of being left alone and I'm afraid of never knowing friendship and I'm afraid I'll lose my way and never find the safety of myself again. I want to touch you, world, and feel your pulse surge and hear your laughter and see your beauty and share your heartbeat and become a part of you. I want to touch you, world, but I don't want to leave my shell, for it's far too safe and warm and soft in here and I don't know if I'm ready for you yet. So, let me test you, world, please, just to see if there's a place in you for me.

Here again we see it—the deep yearning of a person to touch the world and experience life, but afraid, afraid of the risks, the demands, the responsibilities.

Does that sound at all familiar to you? It does to me. It reminds me of something I have felt before. And it reminds me of something in the Bible. Isn't this precisely what Jesus' parable of the talents in Matthew 25 is all about?

Remember it with me. One day Jesus told the story about a man who was about to make a trip to a far country. Just before leaving, he called in three of his servants and gave them oversight of his money. To one he gave five talents, to another two talents, and to the last, he gave one talent—and then he left on his journey.

A talent, the largest monetary unit of the day, would have been several years' wages for those servants. The servant with five talents went and traded and gained five more; and the servant with two talents went out and worked and gained two more. But the servant with one talent dug a hole in the ground and hid his master's money because he was afraid he might lose it.

When the master returned, he was delighted with the two servants who had worked and doubled their talents. "Well done, good and trustworthy slave," he said to them, "You have been trustworthy in a few things, I will put you in charge of many things; enter into the joy of your master" (Matt. 25:21). But when the servant with one talent came in and said: "Master, I knew that you were a harsh man, . . . so I was afraid, and I went and hid your talent in the ground. Here you have what is yours" (vv. 24-25).

The master was much displeased. He rebuked the servant, calling him wicked and lazy—and he gave that talent to the one with ten.

Now, what is this story all about? Of course, I know a parable is a story with one central truth, but if I may use poetic language, I would like to point out that there are many fascinating insights here. Let me quickly list a few of them. The parable points out:

1. Mere abstinence from evil is not enough; we must use our talents to do good.

2. If we don't use our gifts, we lose them (ask any musician or athlete or surgeon about that—they know how true that is).

3. Each one of us is unique; every servant receives something, but our talents are different.

4. Life is a sacred trust, and we are accountable to God for it—we are his stewards—we and all we have belong to the master.

5. We are measured not by the amount of our talents, but by what we do with what we have (be sure to notice that the five-talent servant and the two-talent servant received exactly the same reward).

6. We can easily be tempted to be a loser, to bury our talent, to quit on life, to use littleness as an excuse, to hide behind feelings of

inferiority, and to dream of what might have been if only we had been given a little bit more.

Of course, all of these insights are important, but what I want to get to is the question of why the one-talent servant failed. What paralyzed him? What went wrong? Well, he failed because he did nothing but bury his talent. He did nothing because he was afraid! He was literally imprisoned by his own fears.

Now, let's take a look at these fears more closely. We might find ourselves or hear a message from God somewhere between the lines.

First, the One-Talent Servant Failed Because He Was Afraid of a New Idea

As the master goes off into the sunset, can't you just hear the one-talent servant muttering and complaining under his breath: "We never did it this way before." This, of course, is the sin of the closed mind—and, oh, how closed-mindedness does indeed imprison us!

Closed-mindedness—this fear of a new challenge or new idea—has lots of "red-flag sayings" that go along for the ride and expose this weakness for what it really is.

"We never did it that way before" is the classic, but there are many, many others. Do any of these sound at all familiar? "Don't confuse me with the facts!" "I had to hit him quick, he was beginning to make sense!" "You can talk 'til you're blue in the face, but you'll never change my mind!" "I refuse to listen to this!" "I can't! It's impossible!" "There's no way that can be done!" "I've seen lots of changes in my time, and I've been against every one of them!"

The fear of a new idea or a new challenge is a crippling weakness that can slip up on us and imprison us before we know it, and that which began as simple insecurity can all too quickly become a hard, defensive shell, a prison that can smother the very life out of us.

William Barclay, in his *Spiritual Autobiography*, had these scorching words for the closed-minded. He said,

> The only kind of person who really offends me ... is the person with the shut mind who refuses even to think about what is said to him; the person who deliberately misunderstands; the person who substitutes parrot cries for thought and worst of all, the person who criticizes a writer without ever having read a word of his books. I teach to stimulate and awaken and never to indoctrinate and stifle. (Grand Rapids: Eerdmans, 1975, p. 33)

I ran across an interesting story about an experiment done with a type of fish called a pike.

According to this story (dating back one hundred years), the pike may be placed in a tank with a glass partition down the middle and minnows put on the other side. The pike, who loves to eat minnows, will make a desperate attempt to get to the minnows, butting against the glass partition repeatedly for some time. Finally, however, he will give up and stop trying.

The glass partition may then be removed. The pike will now be free to eat the minnows, but a strange thing will have happened. The pike will have gotten it into his mind that the minnows are not available for food.

He will swim in and around those little fish; he will bump into them and brush against them, but he will not eat them. He will starve to death first, the researcher said, because he is "frozen in" on the idea that the minnows are not available to him. His mind is closed ("Scientific Fish Story," *The New York Times*, August 25, 1901).

That story makes an interesting point. You see, life is a sumptuous banquet to those with open minds, minds open to new truth, new opportunities, new experiences, and new challenges. But those who are closed-minded starve to death because they are imprisoned by their own fear of new ideas and new ways. Those who fear a new challenge are locked in a room with open doors. That was the one-talent servant's problem. He failed because he was afraid of a new challenge. Is it your problem as well?

Second, the One-Talent Servant Failed Because He Was Afraid He Wouldn't Do as Well as the Others

He was afraid he wouldn't measure up, afraid he might be outdone or shown up by the others; he was afraid of "loss of face." So, he refused to play the game. Like a child, he jumped on his tricycle and went home. It still happens.

I'm thinking of a man I know in another state who is a fine singer. He has an excellent tenor voice, but he has not sung in church for more than thirty years. Thirty-three years ago, he was active in his church's music program, sang in the choir, and was the church's main soloist.

But then a new singer moved to town. The choir director graciously invited the newcomer to sing a solo, and the new singer did well. The main soloist couldn't stand it. He couldn't bear to hear people compliment the new singer, so he quit the choir.

The choir suffered his loss for a while, but soon enough, others took up the slack. None of us is indispensable; the church rolls on.

But that man has sulked and seethed and buried his talent for thirty-three years. He doesn't come to church much anymore, and when he does come, he sits in the congregation with bitterness written all over his face.

He is mad most of the time. He is cynical and critical of the church, especially the music program, but people long ago stopped listening to him. Here is a man who has wasted his talent and who has wasted thirty-three years. Think of what he has missed while making himself miserable—all because he was afraid he wouldn't do as well as others.

That kind of fear leads to bitterness, self-pity, jealousy, envy, and resentment. That kind of fear is so debilitating and so unnecessary.

We don't have to outdo other people. All God asks is that we be the best we can be. In his classic poem, "Be the Best of Whatever You Are," Douglas Malloch puts it like this:

> If you can't be a pine on the top of the hill,
> Be a scrub in the valley—but be
> The best little scrub by the side of the rill;
> Be a bush if you can't be a tree.
>
> . . . .

If you can't be a highway, then just be a
    trail,
If you can't be the sun be a star;
It isn't by size that you win or you fail—
Be the best of whatever you are!

Don't let the fear that you might not do as
well as others imprison you.

Third, the One-Talent Servant Failed Because He Was Afraid of Work

His master called him slothful. But, you
know, I think it runs deeper than just plain old
laziness. The real tragedy of the one-talent servant is not that he buried his gift and made no
money. The real problem was that he had no
sense of purpose.

People with a purpose are never lazy. Their
work becomes an exciting expression of their
faith and cause. A good case in point is Mother
Teresa.

Mother Teresa worked for many years with a
leper colony called the Home for the Destitute
and Dying. Her work was zestful and vibrant
because she saw Christ in it so vividly.

She pretended that every person she met was
Christ in disguise! Why don't you try that
sometime? It will change your life. Here is

Mother Teresa's daily prayer. She called it "Jesus, My Patient."

> Dearest Lord, may I see you today and every day in the person of your sick, and, whilst nursing them, minister unto you. Though you hide yourself behind the unattractive disguise of the irritable, the exacting, the unreasonable, may I still recognize you, and say: "Jesus, my patient, how sweet it is to serve you." Lord, give me this seeing faith, then my work will never be monotonous. I will ever find joy in humoring the fancies and gratifying the wishes of all poor sufferers. O beloved sick, how doubly dear you are to me, when you personify Christ, and what a privilege is mine to be allowed to tend you.

How is it with you? Do you have that kind of purpose in your work? Or are you like the one-talent servant: locked in a prison of boredom and laziness and emptiness?

Finally, the One-Talent Servant Failed Because He Was Afraid to Act

There are some people who know that there is something they ought to do, but, like the one-talent man, they are afraid to act.

I'm thinking of the father who knows he ought to spend more time with his children, but somehow he never gets around to it.

I'm thinking of those persons who are suffering the pain and hurt of a broken relationship. They know it needs to be set right, but they are afraid to act.

I'm thinking of that couple who know that communication is breaking down in their marriage, but they just let it go and continue to drift apart.

I'm thinking of those people who know they ought to come on and join the church but continue to put it off.

And I'm thinking of those people who have dropped out of the church and who know they need to come back, but somehow they are afraid—afraid to act—and they are imprisoned by their fear.

Listen! Is there something in your life right now that needs fixing? Is there something you need to do, some word you need to say, some commitment you need to make?

Well, what's the holdup? What are you waiting for? Why do you keep putting it off? Why do you keep burying it in the ground? If you will try, God will help you.

Some years ago, I attended a workshop at Lake Junaluska in North Carolina. The closing worship service ended with a moving responsive reading. The responsive reading, written by Charlene Anderson, was in the form of a dialogue between God and the worshipers. As the dialogue begins, God is calling us to serve him in the deep places of life, and we are responding to his call (at first) with some fear and anxiety. But God keeps reminding us of his strength and dependable presence, assuring us that he will always (in every circumstance) be there for us. God calls us to come on out into the deep water, but we make our excuses: We are not great swimmers. We are not sure we can make it that far. There might be a dangerous undertow that will sweep us away. Our feet can touch the bottom where we are now. We feel safe and secure in this shallow place. We are afraid and uncertain. But God keeps calling us to come out farther because the deep belongs to God. And still we procrastinate and hesitate. We feel inadequate. We feel all alone. God reassures us that we can do it and then says: You are not alone. I am with you. And the dialogue ends as we say in faith: OK, Lord, here we come!

5

The Priority of Forgiveness
"Why Should We Forgive?"

Scripture: Matthew 18:21-35

A little boy had accidentally broken his sister's favorite doll. He really was sorry about it and told her so, but she was too mad to listen. He begged her forgiveness, but she would not forgive him. Finally, their mother intervened, saying, "Now, Sally, it was an accident. Your brother didn't mean to break your doll. He said he is sorry. You will forgive him, won't you?" Sally answered, "Oh, all right, I'll forgive him, but I could forgive him a lot easier if I could slug him one first!" Sally expressed something that we all know full well, namely, that sometimes it's hard to forgive. Yet the Scriptures are very clear about this. When it comes to forgiveness, we as Christians are called to imitate the forgiving spirit of God. The Scriptures point out very dramatically that we are to forgive others as graciously, as lovingly, as mercifully, as thoroughly, as God forgives us. Jesus sums it up in the sixth chapter of Luke with these words: "Be merciful, just as your Father [in heaven] is merciful" (v. 36). And in the eighteenth chapter of Matthew, Jesus underscores again the importance of the forgiving spirit with this fascinating parable that we traditionally call the parable of the unmerciful servant.

First, remember the setup of the parable. Jesus has been teaching the disciples, warning them against self-centeredness, which brings division and makes people quarrelsome, judgmental, and unforgiving. Then Simon Peter steps forth and asks an interesting question: "How often," he says, "should I forgive?" (v. 21).

We owe a great debt of gratitude to Simon Peter and his brash tongue. Over and again Peter rushed into speech or blurted things out and often put his foot in his mouth, and his impetuosity prompted immortal teachings from Jesus. On this occasion, Simon Peter is actually trying to impress Jesus. He asks Jesus how often we should forgive, and then he answers his own question by suggesting that we should forgive seven times.

Of course, Simon Peter knew the law of the day: forgive a first offense, forgive a second, and a third, but then punish the fourth. Peter, wanting to show his magnanimous spirit, goes on beyond the Talmud and asks, "[Shall I forgive] as many as seven times?" (v. 21).

Peter was hoping for a "gold star" with that answer.

But Jesus surprises him by pointing out that forgiveness should be unlimited: "Not seven times, but, I tell you, seventy-seven times," he says, and what Jesus means by that is "Forgive an untold, never-ending number of times." The number seven was, for the Jews, the number of perfection. When time has run through seven days, it begins again, the circle is complete. So we see that no expression could more forcibly convey that forgiveness is to be unlimited than this "seventy-seven times."

Forgiveness is not a matter of arithmetic. It's not a matter of asking how many times must I hold off before I hit back. No, forgiveness is an overflowing spirit. It keeps no score of wrongs.

It holds no grudges. It is being merciful, just as God is merciful.

So, if you ever wonder, "Should I forgive that person who has wronged me or hurt me?"—if that question ever comes to your mind—remember that forgiveness is one thing that is always right. And remember that being Christian means being Christlike, and that means to have his forgiving ways.

Second, look specifically at the parable now. This parable of the unmerciful servant illustrates dramatically the beauty of forgiveness and exposes dramatically the ugliness of the unforgiving spirit. Notice that this parable is like a one-act play with three distinct scenes. Think of it like that. Imagine now that the curtain goes up on scene one. A king is center stage, taking inventory of his kingdom, settling accounts with his servants. A servant is brought before the king. This servant owes ten thousand talents, and he cannot pay it back. Notice here the amount of the debt—10,000 talents. This is a whopping big debt! Myron S. Augsburger, in his book *The Communicator's Commentary: Matthew* (Waco: Word Books, 1982), states that this debt is worth approximately $12 million! A gigantic amount of money! A tremendous indebtedness! Let me illustrate how big this debt is with a few examples.

First, in the first century, a young slave could be bought for one talent (about twelve hundred dollars), and this servant owes the king ten thousand talents, the equivalent of ten thousand slaves.

Second, if this debt were put into coins it would take eighty-six hundred people to carry it all, with each carrying sixty pounds of coins. And the carriers would form a line five miles long. We are talking big money here!

Also, at this time, the total amount of the annual taxes for the five geographical regions of Judea, Idumea, Samaria, Galilee, and Perea (all totaled together) came to only eight hundred talents. And, here, this one servant owes ten thousand talents—millions of dollars—and he can't possibly pay it back.

So, he pleads for mercy, he acknowledges his great debt, and he pleads for forgiveness. Amazingly, the king, who is a gracious man, is moved with compassion; his heart goes out to this servant, and he releases the servant, he forgives him. Incredibly, the gracious king cancels his enormous debt and sets him free! And with that, scene one comes to a close.

Now the curtain goes up for scene two. Same play, second scene, and this time the shoe is on the other foot: the servant whose great debt was canceled by the king in scene one becomes, in scene two, a creditor, a man of power, the one to whom money is owed. As this "forgiven servant" comes out of the palace (a great burden lifted, a free man, a new man, a forgiven man), he sees a fellow servant who owes him money— a hundred denarii (or in our terms, about twenty dollars). Now picture this: the servant who has just had his twelve-million-dollar debt forgiven sees a man who owes him twenty dollars. What does he do? He grabs him by the throat and says, "Pay me what you owe. Give me my twenty dollars now!" This fellow servant falls on his knees and pleads for mercy. But the unmerciful servant, who has only moments before received forgiveness from the gracious king, has no mercy to give; there is no forgiveness in his heart, and he sends his fellow servant to prison. Here, in scene two, we see the graphic ugliness of the unforgiving spirit. Here we see dramatically how ungrateful and mixed up we can become when we accept God's gracious forgiveness and then refuse to forgive others, refuse to live in that spirit. And here scene two comes to an end.

Now the curtain opens for the last scene, scene three. The king is again center stage. A group of servants come in to him filled with distress. They report what the unmerciful servant has done. The king is not happy. He calls in the unmerciful servant and rebukes him. "What's this I hear? I forgave your debt. Should you not have had the same kind of mercy on your fellow servant?" Then the king casts the unmerciful servant into prison, and the final curtain comes down. The play is over.

Let me list a few thoughts about what we can learn from this parable, and, of course, you will think of others.

The Parable Shows Us How Forgiveness Comes About

This parable shows clearly that forgiveness is a gift. It can't be earned; it can't be bought—it can only be given by the one who has been wronged. Let me show you what I mean.

A few years ago, I received a long-distance, collect call from Boston. I accepted the call because I recognized the name of the young man calling. His name was Brad. He was seventeen years old, a runaway. A year or so before, Brad had been left in charge of the family store, and that night (after a heated argument with his dad) he had emptied the cash register, robbed his own family, and run away. His family had not heard from him for more than a year.

On the phone that morning he said, "Jim, I want to come home! I'm so ashamed of what I have done to my family. I'm really sorry and I want to come back, but I don't know if my folks will forgive me, and I wouldn't blame them if they didn't. I know I don't deserve it, but I'd like to have another chance. Can you help me?" We agreed that I would talk to his parents and get their answer, and that Brad would call my office at four o'clock that afternoon for the verdict.

That afternoon at exactly four o'clock, the phone rang. When I answered it, Brad didn't even take the time to identify himself, he was so anxious that he blurted out, "What did they say?" I said, "Just a minute, Brad. There's someone here who wants to speak to you," and I handed the phone to his father. I'll never forget what his father said: "Son, we want you to come home. We've looked everywhere for you. I'm so glad to hear your voice. I'm so glad you're safe. You know, of course, that you have hurt us deeply, our hearts have been broken, but we love you, and we forgive you. Your mother and I will be on the next plane to Boston. We are coming to get you and to bring you home."

That's how forgiveness happens—the only way it happens—as a free gift from the one who has been wronged. It can't be earned or bought. It's a gift. In this parable in Matthew 18, God is the gracious king who freely cancels our debt, who freely forgives, not because of our goodness but because of his goodness, mercy, and unconditional love.

The Vengeful, Unforgiving Spirit Is Dangerous and Destructive, and We Are Answerable to God for It

Our hateful, condemning judgments boomerang; they come back to haunt us. Over and over the Scriptures tell us that. But when will we ever learn? Don't miss this now. Be sure to note here in the parable that the unmerciful servant ends up in prison not because of his debt to the king but rather because of how he treated his neighbor, how he dealt with his fellow servant. This is a judgment parable. However we may imagine the judgment, this parable (along with others Jesus told) makes a very significant point: somewhere, somehow, sometime, we have to stand before God and answer these questions: "How did you treat your neighbor?" "How did you deal with your brothers and sisters?" The message is clear: we can't come into the presence of God with hatred or vengeance in our hearts. Fellowship with a merciful God is only possible for a merciful person.

It happened at recess at an elementary school. Tom bumped into Jack and knocked Jack down. It made Jack so mad that he was determined to get Tom back. All day long, Jack plotted his revenge. Finally, he decided to find a rock and carry it in his pocket, and the next time he saw Tom he would hit him with it. That would teach Tom a lesson. Jack was proud of his plan. Early the next morning, Jack found the perfect rock. It was rough and jagged, just what he needed. He put it in the front right pocket of his jeans and went off to school looking for Tom so he could get his revenge. But, Tom had the flu and didn't make it to school that day. For every day the rest of that week, Jack carried the rock in his right front pocket, but Tom was still not in school. Then on Friday night, as he prepared to go to bed, Jack took off his jeans only to discover that his leg was bruised and scraped and bleeding. The jagged rock, the object of vengeance he had carried in his pocket all week, had injured him! That's the way vengeance works. It hurts us more than it hurts others. The vengeful, unforgiving, hateful spirit is so destructive and so dangerous and so un-Christian.

Now, one final word.

The Main Point of the Parable Is That God Is Gracious, Merciful, and Forgiving, and He Wants Us to Be That Way Too

He wants us to imitate his forgiving spirit. He wants us to receive his gracious gift of forgiveness and, then, to pass it on to others.

Our young people sing a song about that. This popular song, called "Pass It On," describes how just a small spark can create a beautiful glowing campfire that can warm all those around it and how that spark is a dramatic symbol of God's gracious and merciful love. The song ends with this powerful and relevant point: Once we have truly experienced God's forgiving love, we are so bowled over by his unconditional love and forgiveness that we can't sit still. We want to pass it on. In other words, God is gracious, merciful, and forgiving toward us, and he wants us to be that way toward others. He wants us to receive his love and then to pay it forward, to share it with others, or, as the song puts it, to pass it on.

6

The Priority of Strong Foundations
"Building on the Rock"

Scripture: Matthew 7:21-29

Some years ago, in a small town in central Europe, a visitor saw something that fascinated him, something that seemed very strange to him. He noticed the native villagers performing the same highly unusual ritual. As they passed by a certain ordinary-looking wall, they would nod casually in the direction of the wall and then make the sign of the cross as they walked on by.

Some would be walking briskly, others more slowly, but they all did the same thing: they would nod at the wall and then make the sign of the cross as they passed by. When the visitor asked why they did this, no one knew. "We've always done that," they said. "It's a tradition, a time-honored ritual in our village. Everybody does it. Always have."

The visitor's curiosity got the best of him and he began chipping away at the layers of paint and dirt covering the wall until, underneath, he discovered a magnificent mural of Mary and the baby Jesus! Generations before, the townspeople had had a beautiful reason for bowing and making the sign of the cross at that place. It had been an altar of prayer in the heart of the village.

But succeeding generations didn't know that; they had only learned the ritual. They continued to go through the motions without knowing the reason. They performed the practice, but it had absolutely no meaning for them and had no impact on their lives at all. That's an appropriate parable for many people today in their approach to religion, isn't it?

Their faith experience is not much more than a vague nod in God's direction. They casually perform some of the rituals of faith, but they don't really know why, and the rituals have become so routine, so casual, so matter-of-fact, that there is no power, no strength, no inspiration in them at all—a little nod here, a token gesture there, but no depth, no spirit, no life!

But in the Sermon on the Mount Jesus shows us dramatically that this kind of shallow, non-chalant approach to faith won't work. There are storms ahead; the rains of trouble will fall; the floods of stress will come; the winds of challenge will lash against us. Shaky, unstable, wobbly, wavering, casual, routine faith won't hold together. The storms of life will rip that apart and smash it to the ground. We need a strong and stable house of faith built on a rock-solid foundation!

Here's how Jesus put it. He said,

> Not everyone who says to me, "Lord, Lord," [that is, not everyone who makes a casual nod in my direction] will enter the kingdom of heaven, but only the one who does the will of my Father in heaven.... Everyone then who hears these words of mine and acts on them will be like a wise man who built his house on rock. The rain fell, the floods came, and the winds blew and beat on that house, but it did not fall, because it had been founded on rock. And everyone who hears these words of mine and does not act on them will be like a foolish man who built his house on sand. The rain fell, and the floods came, and the winds blew and beat against that house, and it fell—and great was its fall! (Matt. 7:21, 24-27).

Now, what is this rock-solid foundation that Jesus is talking about here? Well, this is the conclusion of the Sermon on the Mount, and he is obviously referring to what he has just taught in the preceding chapters. He says it: "Hear these words and do them and you will be wise and strong, but if you hear these words and don't do them, you will be foolish and weak" (author's paraphrase).

Now, when we go back and read through the Sermon on the Mount carefully, we discover several recurring and dominant themes. Let me underscore three of them.

First, There Is Rock-Solid Commitment

All through the Sermon on the Mount, there is the call to commitment. "Be peacemakers." "Let your light shine." "Enter the narrow gate."

Do you have a rock-solid commitment? Be honest now. How would you rate your commitment to Christ?

On a scale of one to ten, with ten being absolutely terrific and one being very poor, how would you rate your commitment to God and the church? Are you a ten? A nine? An eight? Really? Are you a seven? A four? A two? How would you rate your commitment to God right now?

Do you really put God first in your life? Do you really love him with all your heart, soul, mind, and strength? Are you really committed to God's kingdom and to the doing of his will? Are you really committed to living daily in the spirit of Christ? Do you really love that person sitting next to you right now as much as you love yourself? Are you wholeheartedly committed to supporting the church and upholding the church with your prayers, your presence, your gifts, and your service?

In this great parable, which serves as the conclusion of the Sermon on the Mount, Jesus points out vividly that a commitment built on shaky, shifting sands will not work. A rock-solid commitment is needed. An unflinching, unwavering commitment to Christ is what we must have to stand against the treacherous storms of life.

Some years ago, I received a call one morning from some dear friends. "We've just received the results of Mom's tests," they said. "It's bad news—real bad. She has six months to a year to live, and we want you to come and tell her the situation." Her name was Marjorie, and she was fifty-seven years old. When I got there, she was seated by the window in the den watching her granddaughter playing in the backyard. As I sat down with her, I was trying to figure out how to say it—how to tell her—and this conversation took place:

"Well, Jim," she said, "looks like you drew the short straw. I know that you've come to give me the bad news."

"Well," I answered, "I do have the results from your tests."

"How long do I have?" she asked.

"Now, Marjorie, you know it's hard to be precise on these things, but the doctors say six months to a year."

"I'm not surprised," she said. "That's about what I expected." We were quiet for a moment and then I asked, "Marjorie, how do you feel inside right now?" She said, "When I look out there and see my granddaughter, I feel like crying." And I told her I felt like crying too, and we did cry a little, but then she said, "Jim, I'm not afraid. All my life I've gone to Sunday school and church. I'm a believer! I'm committed to Christ with every fiber of my being. Christ has been my savior in this life. He will be my savior in the life to come. I believe that with all my heart, and I'm committed to him heart and soul!"

Now, let me ask you: are you committed to Christ like that? Is your commitment that strong? Marjorie had built her life on the solid rock of commitment, and when the storm came, that rock-solid commitment served her well.

Second, There Is Rock-Solid Trust

This, too, is a prominent theme in the Sermon on the Mount: Don't be anxious. Don't be fretful. Don't be afraid. Just seek first God's kingdom and his righteousness. Let God rule in your life. Trust him and things will fall in place for you.

The artist Rembrandt once painted a piece titled *Storm on the Sea of Galilee*. It's a remarkable work of art for two reasons. First, it's a Rembrandt—an artistic, priceless masterpiece, a portrayal so real you can almost feel the spray of the waves and the movement of the boat.

The second reason this painting is striking is that, as you study the detail, you notice something unusual: not counting Jesus, there are thirteen other men on the boat. Now, wait a minute. Weren't there twelve disciples? You count again—yes, there are thirteen men plus Jesus on the boat—a total of fourteen.

Gradually, your eyes focus on one particular figure on the boat. He is holding on for dear life. Suddenly, you recognize the face. It's the face of Rembrandt. The artist has painted himself into the scene. He is experiencing the storm, and it is frightful. But the good news is Jesus is there! Jesus is in the boat with him. Jesus will save him from the fury of the storm.

The apostle Paul expressed it like this: "I am ready for anything for Christ is with me and He is my strength" (author's paraphrase). Do you have that kind of faith? Do you know firsthand that kind of trust?

William McElvaney once described an interesting thing that happened in church one Sunday morning. It was a small church, and they were having communion. The congregation had been instructed to pass the communion elements down the pew with each person saying the words of administration to the neighbor, "John, this is the body of our Lord given for you," and "John, this is the blood of our Lord shed for you."

But on this day, one man in the congregation who was not liturgically minded turned to his neighbor, handed him the bread, and promptly forgot what he was supposed to say. He just went blank. After a brief but agonizing pause he finally blurted out to the man next to him these words: "Harvey, hang in there!" ("Windows to Truth," July, August, September, 1991).

I've seen a number of different liturgies for the Lord's Supper over the years, and I don't really think the words "Harvey, hang in there" are in any of them. But, actually, I can't think of any better words to say when we are remembering Christ's gift to us, his presence with us, Christ's watchcare over us. What better words could you say than "hang in there"? You can "hang in there" with a rock-solid commitment and with a rock-solid trust, and he will see you through. You can count on that.

Finally, There's a Rock-Solid Love

In a powerful way, Jesus calls for love in the Sermon on the Mount. "Love your enemies. Pray for those who persecute you. Be perfectly loving like God" (author's paraphrase).

John and Margie were married in 1941. They were both tough and rugged people, raised on the farmlands of America. Together, they had big dreams, high hopes of becoming the most successful farmers anywhere in the United States. However, four years after they were married—and after two children—Margie was struck down with polio. She spent the rest of her life in an iron lung. Still so young (just in their 20s), their life dreams were shattered. John had to give up his lifelong dream of being a farmer and come inside and devote his life to taking care of Margie and the children.

Many years later, when John and Margie celebrated their fortieth wedding anniversary, someone asked John how he had done it for all of those years. John answered simply, "I'm a Christian, and we try to keep our promises. And besides, I love her."

A few years later, after Margie died, their son asked John how he had done what he had done all of those years. Again, John's answer was simple, "I never thought about doing anything else. You just do it, and God helps you." (Thanks to Don Shelby for this illustration.)

You know where John learned that kind of sacrificial love, don't you? He learned that at the church. He learned it in the Scriptures. He learned it in the Sermon on the Mount. He learned it at Golgotha. He learned it from Jesus, the king of love.

If you and I will just do it—just build our lives on rock-solid commitment, on rock-solid trust, on rock-solid love—then God will help us. He will be with us. He will give us strength. He will hold us together and enable us to withstand the treacherous, dangerous storms of life. That's what this parable teaches us.

Suggestions for Leading a Study of
Jesus' Parables About Priorities

John D. Schroeder

This book by James W. Moore examines some of Jesus' parables to see what we can learn from them about priorities. This study guide was created to help make this experience beneficial for both you and members of your group. Here are some thoughts on how you can help your group:

1. Distribute the book to participants before your first meeting and request that they come having read the first chapter. You may want to limit the size of your group to increase participation.

2. Begin your sessions on time. Your participants will appreciate your promptness. You may wish to begin your first session with introductions and a brief get-acquainted time. Start each session by reading aloud the snapshot summary of the chapter for the day.

3. Select discussion questions and activities in advance. Note that the first question is a general question designed to get discussion going. The last question is designed to summarize the discussion. Feel free to change the order of the listed questions and to create your own questions. Allow a set amount of time for the questions and activities.

4. Remind participants that all questions are valid as part of the learning process. Encourage their participation in discussion by saying there are no "wrong" answers and that all input will be appreciated. Invite participants to share their thoughts, personal stories, and ideas as their comfort level allows.

5. Some questions may be more difficult to answer than others. If you ask a question and no one responds, begin the discussion by venturing an answer yourself. Then ask for comments and other answers. Remember that some questions may have multiple answers.

6. Ask the questions "Why?" or "Why do you

believe that?" to help continue a discussion and give it greater depth.

7. Give everyone a chance to talk. Keep the conversation moving. Occasionally you may want to direct a question to a specific person who has been quiet. "Do you have anything to add?" is a good follow-up question to ask another person. If the topic of conversation gets off track, move ahead by asking the next question in your study guide.

8. Before moving from questions to activities, ask group members if they have any questions that have not been answered. Remember that, as a leader, you do not have to know all the answers. Some answers may come from group members. Other answers may even need a bit of research. Your job is to keep the discussion moving and to encourage participation.

9. Review the activity in advance. Feel free to modify it or to create your own activity. Encourage participants to try the "At home" activity.

10. Following the conclusion of the activity, close with a brief prayer, praying either the printed prayer from the study guide or a prayer of your own. If your group desires, pause for individual prayer petitions.

11. Be grateful and supportive. Thank group members for their ideas and participation.

12. You are not expected to be a "perfect" leader. Just do the best you can by focusing on the participants and the lesson. God will help you lead this group.

13. Enjoy your time together!

Suggestions for Participants

1. What you will receive from this study will be in direct proportion to your involvement. Be an active participant!

2. Please make it a point to attend all sessions and to arrive on time so that you can receive the greatest benefit.

3. Read the chapter and review the study guide questions prior to the meeting. You may want to jot down questions you have from the reading and also answers to some of the study guide questions.

4. Be supportive and appreciative of your group leader as well as the other members of your group. You are on a journey together.

5. Your participation is encouraged. Feel free to share your thoughts about the material being discussed.

6. Pray for your group and your leader.

Chapter 1
The Priority of Love

Snapshot Summary

This chapter looks at compassion, forgiveness, and redeeming love as qualities that are a reflection of God.

Reflection / Discussion Questions

1. What lessons do we find in the parable of the prodigal son?

2. Share a time when you learned a lesson about the power of love.

3. What is mercy? What does it mean to be merciful?

4. Name some qualities that are reflections of God.

5. Explain the following statement: "To be compassionate means to get into another person's shoes."

6. How does a person become more patient and compassionate?

7. Why is forgiveness better than resentment? Name some advantages.

8. Reflect on / discuss the meaning of redeeming love.

9. Explain how Jesus was both the message and the messenger.

10. How did your reading and discussion of this chapter personally enrich you? What additional insights or questions would you like to explore?

Activities

As a group: Search the Bible for examples of compassion.

At home: Reflect on the power of love and put it into practice this week.

Prayer: *Dear God, thank you for loving us and for being an example of how we are to love others. Help us practice compassion, forgiveness, and redeeming love. Amen.*

Chapter 2
The Priority of Grace

Snapshot Summary

This chapter reminds us of the many forms of grace, including undeserved love, unconditional love, unending love, and unselfish love.

Reflection / Discussion Questions

1. Why is grace often called "amazing"? Give some reasons.

2. Share a time when you experienced grace that was amazing.

3. Explain what it means that God is gracious.

4. What does it mean to make grace a priority? Give an example.

5. Name some times or situations when love is not deserved, but it is needed.

6. In what ways are all Christians like the prodigal son?

7. How would you define unconditional love?

8. Name some common restrictions people often place on giving love.

9. How can we be bearers of God's grace to others?

10. How did your reading and discussion of this chapter personally enrich you? What additional insights or questions would you like to explore?

Activities

As a group: Read the words of the hymn "Amazing Grace" to identify descriptions and truths about grace, God, and love.

At home: Pray about how you can be more of an example of God's grace in the lives of others.

Prayer: *Dear God, thank you for showing us the beauty and power of grace. Help us be gracious and loving. Remind us of your constant presence in our lives. Amen.*

Chapter 3
The Priority of Being Prepared

Snapshot Summary

This chapter reminds us that we need to prepare ourselves spiritually in advance, because in times of crisis, there are some things, like a personal commitment to faith, that we just can't borrow.

Reflection / Discussion Questions

1. Name some things in life that people try to prepare for or anticipate.
2. Describe a time of crisis in your life. Were you prepared or not prepared?
3. What lessons can we learn from the parable of the wise and foolish maidens?

4. Give an example of spiritual poise, and reflect on / discuss how a person acquires it.

5. Explain what the author means by the statement, "You cannot borrow the Bible."

6. How can reading the Bible each day prepare you for crisis?

7. Share a time when prayer helped you through a crisis.

8. Reflect on / discuss what makes the church "the church," and why it cannot be "loaned out."

9. The author points out that "each of us must find his or her own faith." How do *you* find personal faith in God?

10. How did your reading and discussion of this chapter personally enrich you? What additional insights or questions would you like to explore?

Activities

As a group: Create a Spiritual Survival Kit that you could use in times of crisis. What items would you place in your kit, and why? Search the Bible for ways in which Jesus demonstrated spiritual preparedness.

At home: Think about how prepared you are spiritually for a crisis. How might you become better prepared?

Prayer: *Dear God, thank you for reminding us of the wisdom of preparing now for times of crisis. Help us to grow a strong faith now that will help us in times of trouble in the future. Amen.*

Chapter 4
The Priority of Courage

Snapshot Summary

This chapter uses the parable of the talents to show us that because of God, we don't have to be afraid; we can open our minds and our hearts to God's call.

Reflection / Discussion Questions

1. In your own words, explain what it means to have courage.

2. Name some times in life when courage is needed.

3. Complete this sentence: "Being a *Christian* in today's world is like..."

4. What are some of the lessons we can learn from the parable of the talents?

5. Why are some people often afraid of a new idea or a new challenge?

6. Share a time when you were closed-minded and later regretted it.

7. Reflect on / discuss why some people feel they need to outdo others. What standard does God expect of us?

8. What sense of purpose or work motivates you? Share what excites you.

9. What are some of the dangers of our failing to act?

10. How did your reading and discussion of this chapter personally enrich you? What additional insights or questions would you like to explore?

Activities

As a group: Use the Bible to locate favorite verses that give you courage. Share your verses among the group and explain why you have chosen them.

At home: Examine your fears this week and take a step out in faith by doing something that challenges you to achieve your potential in serving God's purpose.

Prayer: *Dear God, thank you for providing all the tools we need to live a life of courage. Help*

us never to be afraid, because you are always
with us. Remind us that we can overcome any
obstacle that comes our way. Amen.

Chapter 5
The Priority of Forgiveness

Snapshot Summary

This chapter uses the parable of the unmerciful servant to remind us to be like God: gracious, merciful, and forgiving.

Reflection / Discussion Questions

1. Share an important lesson you have
learned about forgiveness.

2. Name some reasons why it is sometimes
difficult to forgive.

3. In your own words, what does it mean to
truly forgive someone?

4. What are some of the benefits of practicing
forgiveness?

5. What is needed in order to have our sins
forgiven by God?

6. How does forgiveness come about, according to the parable of the unmerciful servant?

7. In what ways did Jesus model forgiveness in his life and ministry?

8. How can we be injured by failing to forgive?

9. Reflect on / discuss the forgiving spirit of God. What examples of it have you experienced in your own life?

10. How did your reading and discussion of this chapter personally enrich you? What additional insights or questions would you like to explore?

Activities

As a group: Search the Bible for examples of forgiveness and of lack of forgiveness. Talk about your findings.

At home: Reflect upon and pray about your need to be forgiven and to forgive others.

Prayer: *Dear God, thank you for reminding us that forgiveness is a priority. Help us forgive others and ask for forgiveness when needed. Remind us that you are gracious, merciful, and forgiving, and that you want us to be the same. Amen.*

Chapter 6
The Priority of Strong Foundations

Snapshot Summary

This chapter uses Jesus' words from the Sermon on the Mount to show the importance of having a rock-solid commitment, rock-solid trust, and rock-solid love.

Reflection / Discussion Questions

1. Describe some of the difficult times in life when a strong foundation is needed.

2. Share a time when someone stood by you during a stormy time of life.

3. Reflect on / discuss how faith can become weak and lack stability. What are some of the warning signs?

4. What are some signs of a strong and powerful faith?

5. Reread Matthew 7:21-29. What wisdom do we find there in Jesus' words?

6. Reflect on / discuss the importance of having a rock-solid commitment to Christ.

7. How do you achieve a strong trust in God?

8. If someone has a weak faith or foundation, how would you advise that person to repair it?

9. Why is love such an important element of a rock-solid foundation?

10. How did your reading and discussion of this chapter personally enrich you? What additional insights or questions would you like to explore?

Activities

As a group: Create a list of the keys to a strong foundation of faith.

At home: Reflect upon your reading and discussion of this book and how it might serve to shape your life and faith.

Prayer: *Dear God, thank you for this time together and for reminding us of our spiritual priorities. Help us draw closer to Jesus, that we may be an example of God's love to those in need. Amen.*